To Ken + Ho
Hope you enjoy Sam's poetry! Have a wonderful holiday + a great '06.
Much love,
Sydelle
x

MW01200217

3

BODY *of the* WORLD

Sam Taylor

AUSABLE PRESS
2005

Cover art: Paul Klee, "Awakening Woman" *(Erwachende)*
© 2005 Artists Rights Society (ARS), New York / VG Bild-Kunst, Bonn
Bildarchiv Preussischer Kulturbesitz / Art Resource, NY
Author photo by Michele Parker

Design and composition by Ausable Press
The type is Centaur.
Cover design by Rebecca Soderholm

Published by
AUSABLE PRESS
1026 HURRICANE ROAD
KEENE, NY 12942
www.ausablepress.org

Distributed to the trade by
CONSORTIUM BOOK SALES & DISTRIBUTION
1045 WESTGATE DRIVE
SAINT PAUL, MN 55114-1065
(651) 221-9035
(651) 221-0124 (fax)
(800) 283-3572 (orders)

The acknowledgments appear on page 79 and constititute a
continuation of the copyright page.

Library of Congress Cataloging-in-Publication Data

Taylor, Sam, 1975—
Body of the world / Sam Taylor. —1st ed.
p. cm.
ISBN-13: 978-1-931337-28-1 (pbk. : alk. paper)
ISBN-10: 1-931337-26-8 (pbk. : alk. paper)
I. Nature—Poetry. I. Title
PS3620.A967B63 2005
811'6—DC22
2005014473

For my father

BODY *of the* WORLD

CONTENTS

☼

I.

ANONYMOUS

Always I begin before you
like a baker
who has already mixed the sun's first light

into the morning loaf and the smell
of poppyseeds into your sleep

before you wake.

SURFACING

Turning over in sleep, the wavering edges of a body,
delicate as filo dough, the folds
that endlessly encircle—
made of four story buildings;
the hills of San Francisco;
construction workers pacing with orange cones
outside Memphis, a wash of headlights, coffee steam rising
past suede faces;
also the pipes clanking in basements,
lattices of twigs in winter,
peppermint shrimp beneath Atlantic churn
morphing, mid-life, male to female;
and this awareness also, tossed about,
like something drowning, or almost born;
that all of it is one body,
my body. This web of ache that pulls
against the heart, is the heart, the skin,
the world. Also the man asleep
on a grate, Lycea and Grand,
where the merciful steam of hell escapes
to keep him alive, also the waning moon,
the paper napkin in the wind.

ARC

As it is given, it is whispered, it shall be lost.
It begins with your name
and the marble block that becomes your face.
It begins with a city
where your cry is small as the seeds of coriander.

It begins with a claw foot bath and a wind of pine,
mother's black hair,
a flickering streetlight, the waxy yellow skin
of starfruit, and sneaking in
to read your father's manuscript. It begins with seeing a movie

and walking out into a storm. Then everything speeds up.
A jackhammer, lunch counters,
people like a million pebbles, airports, orchids,
dental floss. And soon
you have forgotten that the world is new.

And in the middle, you will be a two piece suit
between traffic signals,
but in the end, the underside of ambrosia
and the breath of green tea.
In the middle, women will come to you naked

with hair clips given to them by their grandmothers,
a sari from the Indian coast,
a limp from when they fell running through the park.
You will watch them try on shoes,
and you will wash them with a vanishing bar of oatmeal soap.

It begins with one woman on a stone bench waiting
beneath a sycamore.
Her body will be filled with torn photographs,
and you will carry them in
and out of Texacos, piece them together by fluorescent light.

When she leaves, it will be because of a complex equation,
a calculus that includes
measurements of how the barges lift the bay, the change
at dusk in children's pockets,
angles of first hallways, additions and subtractions

of plovers, sandpipers. Or something simple and inscrutable
as the surface of a circle—
the digits of pi will follow her down unrepeating streets
past crates of oranges, gaping
mouths of fish, into other rooms, books that you will never read.

Then there will be strangers, elevators, stones scattered in
indoor hotel gardens.
The giant green wings of luna moths, a broom, dust. Maybe
another, hands like
obsolete maps, maybe children, small moons that seem to wane

as your light fades, swallowed into the texture of hay bales,
into the coffee mug light,
the banana leaf light, you will wash the knives, chop cedar. The
          sun will keep setting
deeper in your flesh. And the dark,
the dark light. As it leaves, it will whisper, I was never yours.

REALISM: A LANDSCAPE OF THE BODY
AT ANY LONGITUDE

Feel the old bricks, color of burnt crimson,
and the shipyard ruins, windows shattered; sadness
rolls in off the ocean, you can feel it—

the woman in the motel combing out
her hair before sleep, the faucet drip behind her.
Is it inside or outside? Are you the sea?

Are you the broken board churned against the sea wall?
The octopus' ink? A dying man's
feverous dreams of his wife on shore?

Are you a city filled with streets that do not end
or sleep? Ah, no, you're the one in the museum
sitting quietly before that painting,

finding that when you are moved to cry
the tears are not yours. Rather, they appear there
on that other body, the one standing

alone on the pier, in the corner of the frame.
And when you realize then you must be him
some change falls from his pocket (as he tightens up

his shoe), a key slips through the boards;
he looks up shaking at a moonless sky—suddenly
you watch him realize he is you.

And then you both are gone. No one knows
who keeps walking past the a.m.' s blinking reds,
stopping to gaze in a window at a pecan pie,

or who faces the painting of coffee steaming—
the cream cow beside the napkins, Marilyn
on the wall—who thinks it has been this way forever.

WEDDING SONG

The train was in the station
and an old woman, pale skin and pink dress, white clubbed flowers

drinking ice tea and gin

and earlier another train in the same place
a girl with pig tails eating alphabet soup

and yesterday the same train with a different old woman

split-steel hair dyed to rust, crackers and a crossword,
puzzled. Do I take your hand

not just because it is your hand

but because it is every hand?
As the pigeons store our weight in silver ink wells

and the steel rafters who among us

really knows, touches, tastes, grasps
before we rail and leaf forward, before we feel and fail, unreal,

real and unrail, flailing for words, and back

to the station. It's a man now. And almost dark.
Brimmed hat and *payos*. We are here to meld, to graft, to graph

impossibilities—

an Hasidic Jew cubed in backlit dusk
eating a doughnut

and reading Jonah. Do you agree?

This one bolt shall be
the entire metropolis, the rattling metal of ten thousand feet

the clamor of the calcifying dream

and the quiet window. Sit beside me.
I want to watch the immaculate tv

that plays inside you. The boys, knee-deep in indigo

and almond twilight, dragging in their nets.
The window of that dining car sits empty now.

I will bring you grapefruit in the morning.

THE LOST WORLD

No one speaks the words I need to know.
The name of the tree near the Ventura mission
that lopes and lurches like a drunken dragon
when the wind blows, exposing a sinewed belly
of branches, or the name for when you see the tree
from your car and lower the radio
as if to hear it better, wishing you could
stand still in the street as the car continued
without you, into town, obeying each empty light.

I don't know the words for the wildflowers
that orgasm in this vacant lot, though they've coaxed
my tears with their yellow fingers, their violet mouths.
No one speaks the names of the four-petaled blue compass
or the golden clarinet that turns a man into
a honeybee, and few know. Though any child
will tell you the name of the blinking towers on the hill
or two roads crossing, no one knows
the word for crying and laughing at the same time,

or the verb for two people thinking the same
thought in the same moment—and variations
when it occurs with your lover on a cross-country trip
and you thought she was asleep; another name
when it rises in bed as she dips her chest
into the mirror-water of your face; another word
when you stand together in the kitchen,
slicing carrots and peppers and turn toward each other
in the same instant, and nearly knife each other,

and you start laughing and you do not speak
the thought, because it is everywhere like breath,
like protons, and you know lightning has struck you both,
but also everything—the room, the world. And it is
another thing entirely when you are with your dad
sitting on a mildewed wicker couch in a dark room,
and he is dying, and for a moment you both glow
remembering talks in the woods at night—a flash
of divine mercy, another name no one speaks.

JOHN 3:16

The perfection of God that rose
        Jesus out of its body also put forth
two Mexican girls, four and five, running alone
        down a city street, a wind of white dresses
and red ribbons, hair as fine as black water—
        shouts leaping halfway down the block—
then the mother rounding the corner
        behind them, shaking her head, "They wore me out."

A streak of laughter now. But it could be
        one day mother will be roasting corn
and an uncle will lead one of the girls
        behind a shed—a birthday present he says—

and before she knows how to braid her hair
        or ever hears of Shakespeare, she will tear
her face to shrapnel in the mirror, follow
        any boy who curses down an alley.

That's why he's on the cross. Not for one sin
        or another, but to show us the nature
of birth, to tell himself—his children—the price
        of existence. Because God so loved the world,

he wanted to be a girl with red ribbons,
        a blue Minnie Mouse watch, even if then
he had to forget, to live amongst all the forgetting—
        the tv talk show, the uncle, to watch him each day
through the smell of corn. Because He so loved the world,
        he was willing even to be that fat man

lying on the couch eating *chicharones,*
     scratching his balls, chafed red from the quarry,
because the white light just goes on forever.

HOLOGRAM

When you are sailing and the wind on your brow
makes your outside feel like a blue heart,
don't forget that it's dark inside your pocket
and that the pocket watch that is not there
lies under a glass window in downtown Houston
where a Mexican boy thinks of his grandfather,
points, asks how much it costs. Don't forget
he breakdances in the evening at the Y
and the girl in the corner who just watches
and says "Miguel, you're not using your shoulder"
is also watching you as you suddenly stand
feeling brittle as the cliffs, and so small
a hawk could drag you off. But the girl is happy
to feel the wind on your arm and know there is no end
to the commas in the blue scripture,
though she thinks more often of whether
her parents will be watching television
or fighting when she gets home that night
and of whether or not she is pretty.

ANONYMOUS

The book of your words lies open
on a cafe table
                    beside a glass
of ice, an inch of amber.

Pages turning in the wind.

Now, I am a Venetian boatman.
Now, a Laotian farmer
standing in the doorway, watching the rain.
Now, I press my rifle into a line
of Jews, beg them to move right, then left.
And Mary watches His hand's shadow
fall across the wall
wondering if it will touch hers.

The woman who had been reading there
had to pee, a warm trickle
and thought of the credit card bill
she had to pay and how she needed sandals
and the lighthouse near where she was born
holding her aunt's hand the first time up,
how she collapsed halfway in tears
because it seemed she would never make it.

Sounds of someone entering the next stall.
There was a humming from the air conditioner,
blue and white tiles, lime green panties
arched above her sneakers.

Somewhere in the book this page was buried.
She had found it, and the wind was looking.

II.

LISTEN

I am pushed through a hall in a house of seas.
At the end someone watches my approach;
it is me.
Holding a mountain of salt in one hand,
a bandage in the other,
I am waiting for the wounded to arrive.
No one else is coming.

ACCIDENT

A beacon moving through the darkest crime scene
my friend said when I told him I didn't know
what love was. Two months later, Joel woke up
reclined in a truck that had no doors or windshield,
his left shoe missing, the driver's seat beside him
empty. Somebody was calling his name—

no, not his name, just calling him, so precisely
it tugged his sternum like a name. He rose,
walked around the vehicle—the tires
were gone, two wheels stripped to their axles—
and there she was on the ground, sitting
against the truck, legs outstretched. He felt relieved,

she must have collapsed, pouting at herself,
sheepish for the mess she'd caused. Where was the road?
He heard it humming in the distance. He leaned down
to her, but she did not move. He was terrified then
of the silence he felt that moment
which was not the quiet of trees or the moon

or of hot tea, but the silence of somewhere else,
of a lake being where a girl should be.
I didn't ask him if he saw a beacon in that field,
the windshield shattered sixty yards away,
the sky a frigid wishing well. I imagine
what he would have to say—waking in the twisted metal

dark, walking round the Ford to find her
sitting in the grass, already gone, her suitcase open
fifty feet away. That there was no beacon, just taillights
and windows scattered in the weeds, the truck's steel carcass,
and the stars they had shared, now his alone,
tickling her shell. The beacon was nowhere. He was the beacon

he would have to say, standing alone, his pulse snapping
against the sky, filling the veins of the night,
plasma, cartilage, bone—crying out for her,
her jacket flapping in the bush. He would have to say
that love does not mean preservation alone,
but also creation and destruction, and only then

is a thing complete, is it revealed, like the windshield
shattered sixty yards away, like Somayyah dead,
sitting calmly in the grass, after the truck she crashed
flipped over fifteen times. Some things are impossible
and they come true. Maybe all things. Two days later,
he returned to the road, found a two inch groove

that trailed into the shrub, followed it, picking up
his wallet, a cell phone, her water bottle. A letter
he had written her last summer, half rain-bled. The truck
towed and gone, he found her spilled menstrual pads
still caught in the sumac, left them, sobbing. I imagine
what he would have to say: that there is no thing

that is not a beacon. No thing that is not a flag
in a mute's hand, trying to reach us. Or a window
holding a face. Except in some spots, the face shines through
more than others, like in Somayyah alive,
or like that night as he leaned over her, noticing
her left foot in the grass was bare, like his own,

and two days later—when his father drove him back—
he found, on a sun-washed hill, beneath a tall pine
her boot, standing upright, still laced and tied.

THE SHORE

Before anything is remembered
water has already decided never to die
then the blood falls

sealed in white rocks
the blood of the sea begins
cold and clear as
a pair of hands
rising
a life ahead of us

then the sand falls

it climbs the sound of water
spiraling inward
until it covers its blue heart

until some morning there is only the shore
and the water and the absence
of something that came
before years

there the names fall

beside the peddler of minds
who waits with his wares
draped in the sun
whistling
and counting the shape of water

all along the coast
destinies set out towards him

knowing only the sound of the sea

MATINÉE

It was on a movie screen. How like gods we are,
          watching a movie, except we remain
corporeal—toes clenched, fingers with nothing
          to claw, except themselves, the table.

On the screen, a red field, brimming
          with hives of black-rimmed blisters, charred
craters, crisped void. I thought of a country
          burning, bombed—men with one shoe

vanished, toeing that ancient pattern of grief—
          a thin wire hung between horizons—
two boys tugging at a mule, a woman holding a blanket
          and a violin, and the wing-air-helpless-beating

chickens scattering like yeast, ten feet high
          against a sky of planes—wasps
in the flowers. We were in the back room
          of a hospital, the screen not much bigger

than a tv, my mother
          and I, watching magnified slides
of her blood. Field after field of silk
          globular red blood cells, gashed

open like the burnt fringe of an egg
          fried over easy, we waited, black eyes
staring back, from a timelessness
          of bat droppings. Finally there entered,

moving among the small red henchman,
      a white queen   quivering
with unfathomable light, like a chorus
      of a thousand diamonds, given life,

more intelligent than any book
      ever written, it was breathing,
it could pray, it could almost speak,
      to the savages it touched, of salvation.

It was the most beautiful thing
      I'd ever seen. I knew then
what the heart was—this city of pulsing suns
      that held the dreams of every one-armed man—

and I knew it was losing. Cracking, breaking.
      I knew it was being driven down
into the earth, that it would split open,
      like a white acorn, spill back

into the cold spaces of soil. It would forget itself,
      its name, its town, the way each of its children
preferred pasta sauce, paella, latkas—
      how to drive a car, how to fold

the laundry, how to catch a newborn's head.
      And I am still there in that room,
beginning to accept that it is so,
      telling myself it will return,

stepping out of that dark bath—
        its light brighter, its code finer—stepping
into hands that will become hands
        a heart that will learn it is a heart,

I am still there, saying goodbye
        to mother
and the white light in her blood
        and the families vanished into the hills

learning to say goodbye
        and come back,
come again,
        in any form.

SONNET IN A MINOR

Of all the Cartesian fields of sorrow

a bowl overflowing with yellow
oranges

Names in mist at the edge of tongues

A fishing rod leans on the rail of a pier

waiting for a person I will never be
Come dear

which memory should we retrieve

Everything lives in the mountains now

even my reflection in airport windows
when she called to say she had to die

Monks eating rice beyond goat trails
and in the rain between cedars, your dorm walls

our first kiss ringed with mercury

SUNDAY MORNING

So she was considering the notion that suffering
was always equal, a universal constant
over breakfast—cereal, banana, orange juice—
coffee? Why not. Nature had its habits: pi,
the golden rectangle, the speed of light; her last lover
wouldn't call for two more days. Pigeons outside

were rehearsing 1917 again, or was it
17 AD—the same innovations, the waddle,
the peck. Jesus walking among them
would have had acne then, full-blown craters,
bluffs, peaks. No less a trial than the desert?
Mortification. She remembered the revelation

in the shower after her mother died
that scars were not unbeautiful, that pain
could not destroy her, might not be painful,
and if she didn't mind what sharp paste
was pressed from her heart—garlic or tears—
she could throw herself into the scalding

water easily as sampling mango salsa
or staring into the magnets of a hard man's eyes.
The burn from a pot of rice, if she listened,
might release a child trembling at the tip
of her finger. A scene might recompose itself—
the pier, his crooked member, cadmium stains

on a cobalt sea—one lone sailboat, sienna speck,
that seemed not to move at all. For weeks,
becoming animal, she'd suddenly leap
into the air kicking, or sensually cling to a wall,
rubbing away the violent insistence on order,
a calm close to death. So when a nail pricked her foot,

she thought she saw Sitting Bull in Central Park.
And when her windshield rained upon her,
it was what men call soul that rose around her,
luminous in all things: the steering wheel, the endless screech
of metal—at the center, a luminous grief,
so luminous it almost burned with pleasure—

and her skin, angelic, barely scratched with blood.
As the moon's cervix dilated, her room took on
a smell—of tears, a lover thought at first, or period—
but it was unmistakably the sea, a flood
had risen about her on all sides, nothing was as it was,
she found liquified and hardened herons

calling from cold tile, brigades of migrant workers
moving through her bed. Her life swam back to her
transformed—and she, the crashing grace of water.
She the flood, the flight, the flood. Above the highest crags.
And then one day it set her down: a couch in Manhattan,
in a still beige room. And now she walks

between the traffic and the storefront window.
And she knows she'll drink wine tonight by stereo,
and kiss a stranger's almost chiseled jaw. She has
all her bills and errands fisted in her mind.
Among the sirens and the linens in the breeze,
she rubs again the pink hypothesis: that pain

is always equal to the height of the horizon.
A problem of perspective. The challenge: first,
she dwells above the fourteenth floor. She never saw
the sounds scrubbed from gas chamber walls,
never drew water from the well after the death squads
had rounded up the men. Nor can her mind rehearse

a happy childhood. She knows she might be wrong.
She puts her paper down, feels flurries of not enough.
Her coffee tastes vacant, its texture nervous.

HERE IN THE MOUNTAINS

Here in the mountains, we remember
there are answers that do not reach us
in the city. Messages of wind, handed
down from leaf to leaf across the hills
of the elders; messages that die
crossing the rivers of pavement,
the oblivious thunder of engines,
the quiet knives of the clocks.

There is a peace that eyes us from a distance,

like coyotes that drop down the mountain
and pause near the edge of town
to hear the choking cries of men
darken the valley of well-lit Nothing,
before returning to the magic
of the hills, the mint and eucalyptus,
the arms opening without end—
the bonfire of silence.

FOR LOVE

I.

There are many things I know are part of me
that I've never seen—like the sweet onion
grass on a French hillside, or the oval-orange
mushrooms that surge there in the muddy
footprints of a goat. But they're not all pretty.
There are great sheaves of blood reamed down
from the necks of pigs and calves, and whole
Philippine seas exploded by dynamite, coral
and fish floating belly up. Also, electric cattle
prods rammed inside Tibetan nuns, and screams
like ribbons in the wind, like leaves
in some countries, like grass. Beside the pecan trees
looking deeply through all the parts of me, she said
I don't believe in pain, and I loved her for that.

II.

There is darkness stored up in the eyes
of humans, more than any bees have honey.
Who can say how it happens? How long
it must lie in that damp cellar—the temperature,
the conditions? A long cold, a brief thaw?
How long alone in the white mountains,
how many days walking under scaffolding
past the legless beggars? It can't be hurried,
predicted. Only sometimes suddenly it happens,
in some man or woman, the darkness
crystallizes, turns from the inside out
into light, a silent vociferous radiance
moving like sap over trees and trash cans
through the body of the endless streets.

AFTER CHARON: A LATE AUBADE

Lake River Mirror-water   Yes come in
we can meet on the other side
of the obvious—the cerebrally palsied head
immortalized at fifty-five degrees,

the wet spiderwebs and cherry blossoms,
the rain crystalline by streetlight,
the wheat in its monk's robes silently climbing
its spiral stairs. So we open up the palm

we open up the chest. We say *these*
are the rivers and the way home. We say
at dusk my grandmother sat in a maple chair
and ate cantaloupe. We say *my you sure are*

a horny bitch today. When death comes
we wear white paint and trousers
we run through the peat bogs, wailing
we climb the sides of wet brick

like orange-colored snails, coffee-colored
snails. We sit and ask to hear
the piano. After a long time
among broken stalks of sugarcane,

we hear the geese again
skimming over the surface of the world—
the fisherman unpacking his catch
over ice at the market, green peppers

sizzling at the taqueria. A little girl
rings the bell on her bicycle.
The Redskins make it to the Super Bowl.
We sleep inside a marble sun.

BACKGROUND

It's possible that was him. The man on the bench
outside the darkened store, beneath a light, reading.

A tightly rolled chrysalis of olive green
an armslength away, and closer at his side,

a stack of newspapers neatly tied with fraying twine
that he must have accumulated over years,

maybe states. What if that was him
you just passed? So meticulous and dignified

in his fate, he sat, as if keeping watch
over the whole brusque, swooned, seasick, siren night,

which somehow took place entirely in his hand,
in the book he held intently—as if he might

be responsible for each person walking through
its pages, each gray moth blended into the asphalt—

the page he held like an eyelash, then turned
slowly as if reliving all its contents once more, in unison,

before proceeding. What was time to him?
His long white hair combed and lightly oiled,

an old suit eerily unwrinkled, glowing
in that one light among shadows, set back from the road,

as if he'd been on that street forever
or had just stepped out of a bath of milk and vetiver

and centuries, his every moment only a matter of being
somewhere. From forty yards, all you could make out

was the broken right margin—poetry? It's possible
that was him, that was God you walked past,

sitting in his garden. It's possible he's in every scene—
the thin, curly haired autistic man ticking wide-eyed

like a lightning rod in the corner of McDonald's,
the plump, dark-haired woman in janitor blue

behind the dumpster and night laurels lifting
almost without movement, almost without anger—

it's possible he's somewhere in every scene,
wandering unnoticed, watching the show, waiting

to see if anyone will recognize him, ask him
"Do you have a light?" or "Want to share my bag of oranges?"

Yes, it's possible you could walk up to anyone—
the pimply youth at Jiffy Lube sweeping

backward through the car lift before dusk
and ask what time they open in the morning

and if you recognize in that moment
what the grease on his cheekbone is made of

as he says seven without turning his head
or just because you have a car and need to change

your oil—even if you don't remember
the ancestry of light—you will be talking to God.

HUMAN GEOGRAPHY

Today I walked over a real mountain.
With real feet. A heart that splashed
in the center of nothing, a red world.

Tonight, I am staying out of the arms
of my love, so I can feel my pain
like a tree standing alone in the night.

＊

Watching the invisible slaves we call
angels haul the clouds over the crest, ropes
taut over their shoulders. Cumulous,

cirrus. Ice slopes like an alphabet
in a land nobody touches. Except like this.
Even the edges of our world are full.

＊

Everyone locked inside a dance. Chained
to the intestinal annelid. To which
has been added the splendor of the dawn,

lichens on the cliff. Who isn't innocent?
Don't make me go out again
into the common language, Lord.

＊

If I can hold the word inside the dreaming
not as an act of certainty, but of
knowing nonetheless—a hand stretched out

in the dark, feeling the stone wall, the plum tree—
the constant rememberance of the fragile
prostrating before us, I can feel calm.

       ✳

Watching invisible angels we call
physics walk the clouds out over the edge
of the world, like a boy walking a horse

to find water—never getting there,
never tiring either. Fall meadow, spring onions.
Nobody knows where they are going.

       ✳

It's time we stopped all the lies. The world
is beautiful. There is nothing to find
more than your own face or hands in the dirt

and the sound of your voice splitting the blue
atom sky, like a raven. Human cry.
Love is nuclear, Mr. President.

       ✳

Let us never say another thing about God
who may favor russet leaf-cutting ants
over the minister or sheik, the aboriginal

above the academic, the woman
to the man. A leaf may be more than a prayer.
Silence might be what words are saying.

      *

It's time we stopped all the lies. The world
is terrible. Placing your hands in your pocket
and breathing as you walk through Wal-Mart

might be the path to salvation. A cell-phone,
a rubber ball, whatever you touch, many have felt
pain, making it, bringing it to you.

      *

Let us never say another thing about God
then we shall see that we cannot speak
again of science or doubt either, but only

of elk stepping through the snowy mountain
and a species of war, spirit-broken,
its metal explosives buried in the good earth.

      *

If we walk on from here, it will be without words
that are meanings, only movements and pictures.
Like a village that has taken what is essential.

The hands that built those ovens are gone now
which means they are in our hands now.
Dig, build, pray. Do. Whatever you can with them.

BRIEF, ACCIDENTAL ORCHESTRAS
found in an attic on 62nd Street

I.

Another hour, I have nothing to say. What is here, the world would not believe. The rain draws circles endlessly in Canadian lakes, interlocking, and a child has fallen asleep on a couch beneath a clock. In his hand, he still holds the shell from the beach, the tideline sweeping over the shore of his mind, erasing with each breath. That's not it though. God is speaking to the woman biting her lip beneath a dripping eave, but how could it be true? God is speaking to the rapist too, but he doesn't want to hear. God is dreaming them both. That's not it either though. If there is a hand, it is every hand. If there is a hand, then there is no hand. And everything in it, flowers.

II.

I speak only on the condition of anonymity, only by the promise that my name will be erased. Then you will understand I spoke the truth, for it was not for my separate kingdom that these words came. These words come from the rivers, the cold slow rivers sweeping over continents, waters separating around the steel hulls of barges and the plastic floaters of old black men fishing with their grandsons. There are endlessly billions of water called molecules—there is one moment when an Iranian girl jumps on top of her father's car. Next door to the crane's half folded wing lives the octave arc of the widow's rocking chair. Most of the people here do not know they are God, and that gives the dream its texture.

III.

It's not like it was before, it's moreso, and it's again. The moon will be reflected in a face. They'll dribble out of the bars, spill a few measures of carbonated speech, this one in the blue jacket will put his arm around that one with a waist of hesitation. The long ago singing in cathedrals, the medieval rain dripping through the roof, will have been for this. And so will the hour of the guy at the print shop making flyers for Renaldo's Pizza—and the boy who twirled them into cylinders and slipped them inside each door handle. Where there used to be questions, now I just see stars in pavement and hear the bar's owner bringing boxes of bottles into the alley, to be recycled.

ORIGINAL SIN

I.
There is no way, as a child, to be prepared
      or to recognize in time to defend ourselves
            that we have arrived in an imperfect world
in which everyone, even those we most love,
      is speckled with some gross failing (forever
            beyond the ken of their rehabilitation)
that requires we strive to understand
      something about their life in order to
            forgive them, like sending out taproots
into the wet or parched soil where they've come from,
      feeling spread toes inside the bamboo
            and the barrel cactus, some fault
that begs we imagine the moon-phase mineral events
      and thoughts settling one by one like feathers
            in the staircase of their spine's logic,
and to do this again and again
      for many seasons, expecting no other progress,
            and we slowly learn to do this
and then only this, because we understand it is necessary
      and that we ourselves require it
            because before we could begin to defend ourselves
from a world of fault, we were already its next of kin,
      its inheritor and progenitor, unwittingly,
            unknowingly at first, and then gradually
awakening one by one to our errors
      as they touched each thing in our house,
            as they bruised, however slightly,
each face we love.

II.
Near the end, when my mother's universe
        was becoming the bedroom of a house she rented
                for her death and also the path
to the bathroom where she'd give herself
        enemas or vomit beside little lavender
                gift soaps and bath salts, a woman named Janice,
who had once been her close friend and then
        had "turned" against her in a power struggle
                among local midwives, returned
and gave my mom an iris plant.
        And it was lovely there beside the bed,
                taking no notice of death, flowering,
as we came and went with carrot juice, smaller
        and smaller portions of food, and then finally
                only chocolate covered almonds,
as faces rose like coins from the bottom of a fountain
        to sit beside her and talk about whatever
                they could think to talk about
with a woman who was dying, the iris
        kept flowering. It seemed almost eternal,
                its purple petals still administering some last rite
of color, when we found her, arm flung-out
        over the bedside, palm upright, in mid-air
                half-fisted beside the iris, as if unsure
whether to release or cling to this world
        as she departed. And two days after the funeral—
                my older sister and I still in that foreign house
packing up the remnants of my mother's life—
        Janice came back. Except, because as a girl Polio
                had nearly killed her, leaving her

obese and crutch-bound, she sent her daughter
          to the door. So that it was her daughter's
                    black hair, soft as riverwater,
that no man had ever grasped as he came inside her;
          it was *her* young eyes, like horses' eyes,
                    that knew nothing of this world
that stood there, while her mother waited   .
          in the mini-van, engine idling,
                    stood there, dutifully, before my sister and me
and asked to have the iris back.

III.

SCULPTURE WITH ONE WING

Oh the body in its bedouin sleep. Always awake,
always walking blocks of city scaffolding,
always wrapped in rain, hot cocoa, cinnamon.
Always a curled embryo, always a curved umbrella,
always the handle of an unknown suitcase,
always the echo that will not fit
inside a cathedral. Always a brief April.

POSTSCRIPT

It's not words we need tonight, but the antidote
to what has already been said. Yes, there's a man
sitting lakeside in an idling car. Yes, there's
a slug crossing a road in the rain, and a drugstore
where people sway like tropical leaves—in a wind
that thinks of antibacterial soap and condoms,
a two-liter of coke. Yes, my father is dying
and the soil turns with its vocabulary
of beetles, its glistening, diamond vowels. Yes,
any face is a temporary face, and God knows
enough about when the mangoes must turn red,
when the garbage man must wake in the dark.
Here. There. A bowl left out in the rain. We fill it
with so many thoughts. As if afraid to merely live
in love. As if even this fear belonged to us.

THE GOSPEL OF J
An Enlightenment Tale

All the vain seekers of glory—
they see His Body hanging there
and miss the other half of the sacrifice.

I gave away my own heart
and for what? A few coins? Mere pretense.
I received Nothing

but the part no one wanted
in the Perfect Story.

When He gave me the bread
my hands shook
just like in the dream
and I remembered how as a child
the anvil
in the corner of my father's room
had always frightened me
as if it might leap into my hands.

I rose without returning any glance
and left the room. I felt betrayed.
It's true, I was never like the others:
Peter and Luke twirling in a wind
of children, while I sat on the rocks
loosening briars from my robe,
trying not to hate them. It was hard
to breathe, hard to walk.

But that day when the soldiers stopped me
in the street and whispered—
yes, for a moment I tingled, moist
with a power I'd always kept away—
then I spit at their feet. I thought
I had triumphed; I didn't understand
why the whole day strangers
seemed to frown at me
from behind baskets of fruit and bullock carts.
And when I entered the room, my master,
who had been all that held me above
all I was, would not look at me.

Outside, it was raining—you don't hear that—
at my hour too, something invisible wept.
I leaned against that wall for hours
wanting to go back in. You see?
That's what I wanted, but for the first time
I was not alone. And everything else
told me to wait.

There were puddles holding reflections of branches
and the sound of metal pounding metal,
the smith still working by his fire.
That's what you have to understand—
it was a normal night. A woman passed
cradling a wrapped bundle to keep it dry.
How could any of this be? She paused
to tuck back in the baby's foot, then was gone.
That's when I realized what I sought
was always mine. That's when I understood
He had to die.

I knew everything
was perfect, but I was a tree of knives
from having fought the world so long.
Suddenly there was no one there
and I saw there never had been.
And yet this body and this story hanging
in midair, trembling, like a bell
ringing the blue night.

What was there to do
but speak to the Pharisees
as if they were real. I walked through the dark, humming
like an impossible river,
past the lanterns in windows,
the sounds of plates,
a quiet squeal, then the silhouettes
of a woman holding a glass
chased by a fat man.
And from a rooftop, someone screamed
(I think) in pleasure.

I knew everything had already been
forgiven. I made a gift of all I had.

WAKING WITH CHLOE
A Suicide's Song

Everything hurts, and she is already awake
naked at the desk, entranced with the rain,
the birch of her back rising like a heron
among reeds. A light has found its way
to the pink of her sex, barely visible,
emerging from its nest, lips pressed against
the cold wood—such quiet where last night
the streets were swallowed by a purple sea,
and she cried words she never had to learn. Lord,
I know there are beautiful things in this world,
but they only make everything hurt worse.

The light that leaves the clouds, diminished,
passes through her body and expands again,
but it doesn't travel far in me, before it dies,
extinguished like a shooting star. In her,
the world turns to watercolor, borders soft
and careless—the birds become branches,
their song, meadows, rolling, rising into
silos. Neither quick nor stupid, she thinks
like the grass that grasps the rain with ten
thousand palms. She doesn't know she's happy.

She loves me, but no differently
than a lily pad or a brightly colored
raincoat. Maybe that's why I loved her,
in the park when I looked up from the juice
I had spilled and found her laughing, as if
I was scenery, an intimate landscape
sliding through her body. I knew her closeness
would not hold me. You see, I'm falling

off this earth, and have been for forty years—
one day, I was feeding hay to my father's
horses, napping in the barn, and the next
I was holding a sign in a crowd, running
from gunfire. The world came to me
in photographs. I tumbled from the nuclei
of atoms through the gallery of eyes turning
welfare lines, and everywhere I saw my own face,
but far off, and through fog, with an undertow
from inside my own blood, dragging me under.

Soon, she will start her stretches, and the light
will bend through her like a prism. When she sees
I am awake, she will jump on my chest
and tease me with color, delicious, acidic;
I will use all my strength to meet her there.
When she rises to make pancakes, I'll slip out
to buy a razor and a bottle of bubbles,
and as we eat, I'll point out
the silkworm cocoons and the dragonflies,
tease her with the sounds she made last night,
watch how her face changes with words and angles.
Then we will blow bubbles in the fields
and I will gaze as she waits, following each
sphere, until it vanishes in some surface,
before blowing again. When we're done,
the sun will be high in the spare laughter
of the oaks, spilling honey, and I will watch
her in that light as long as I can bear.
And then I will send her out to get something.
I don't know what. Maybe flowers. Yes, that's it.

BASICS (1/400TH SHUTTER SPEED)

I love how within the sleep
there is sleep, within the dream

there are dreams, within the story
stories. I try to conceive

how it could be configured so perfectly.
We drink coffee, or we die

with unshuttable eyes in Calcutta.
Women buy tampons and dress in red

leather, or hide themselves
beneath black robes, have orgasms

on hardwood kitchen floors,
shouting "fuck me" in afternoon light,

slip between bamboo stems carrying
machine guns or the dawn's

fistful of eggs. Men rise from under
the hoods of cars, cross rivers

in the dark, eat peanuts between innings,
convince themselves they are important.

They meet, the man and the woman,
around the pool table of Miller's

or behind a church in the jungle.
That night it rains, and her crescendo

that seems as if it might become
everything quickly becomes small

as wet pebbles, underfoot—by day, we hide
in the mountains, we fight for freedom.

Or we come as soldiers with clean boots
dropping cigarettes into the well.

We kill each other, the nautilus grows.
Nothing has ever happened.

THE UNDRESSING ROOM
for Asha Greer

They all had to stand naked there
all ages in front of each other
women, children, and grandmothers—
sunken and budding breasts
      side by side, as if
      each was alone in a room of mirrors

placed at different angles and dates,
reflecting one body through every age,
what she once was, what she might have been,
an illustrated life of the soul's anatomy
      depicted with variances
      for childhoods and chestnut trees,

bowls filled with pears or peas,
a stern father who played the violin,
a kiss beneath the steps of a forbidden
church, all facing the same fate.
      And each knew the feel of the rain
      in the ground beneath their feet,

each was a witness to the brain, each could
recite some text from memory,
the sting of a bee, the call of a lark,
a flint-spark off the heart. Except each stood
      half-atrophied,
      as if the present moment had worn through

every fantasy. In truth, they were not alone—
they were packed like herrings in a tin.
Yet each had to answer for herself
the same question:
        How will I meet my death?
        Will I shriek? Will I scream?

Will I lift up one of the children
and hold her to my chest?
Will I sing? Many of the women sang.
Though there was no reason to sing
        around them were no birds prattling
        in bowers, no milk and honey to bless

just naked bodies and souls squirming
from their defects in the last, unfriendly light
before an asphyxiated death.
Still some sang. They sang for something else,
        something that would not perish
        and had not even been touched

by the gloved hands and secret orders,
the early morning box cars rolling slowly
out of Bialystok through the beech flowers.
That's when the woman telling me
        the story paused and almost smiled
        and came again from a different angle.

Maybe there never is a reason, she said.
I didn't know if she had been there.
She wouldn't tell me, she said it didn't matter.
I knew at least she hadn't died.
>   *Maybe that's the question we answer*
>   *each moment of our ordinary lives.*

In line at the bank, buying milk for the night,
in traffic fumes and ice-sleet storms, siren-breathed:
how will I meet my death? How will I
meet my death? And maybe there never really is
>   *a reason*
>   to sing

even in the arms of our beloved, wife or husband,
even when we're licking
a coconut sno-cone or chocolate torte,
walking into a movie with our popcorn
>   or driving, window-sealed, through the poor
>   side of town, where a black girl turns

and slaps us with a look. How will we
meet our death? . . . And the boys and men
entered that room too, undressed, and squirmed.
Would their humiliation really be
>   their last concern? Would they still pretend
>   not to cry? Some screamed. Some held

a hand. And like the women, many of the Rabbis
sang. Was it that stripped to the bone
they chose to wrap themselves in that clothing?
Or was it that, stripped of everything—
          their clothes, their names, their lives—
          that's what was left, they were, the singing.

NEXT

In one of Barnes and Noble's
windows, I was eating one of Musselman's
applesauces and reading one of Merwin's
poems and watching one of Shiva's
sunsets and thinking one of Sam's

thoughts about how I've come to accept
the writing on the white air,
that I am owned by this name,
a tight knot dragged through centuries
of dust—thinking about words and how

the molecules of a snow flake join hands
to span across the darkness; about cells
dividing at the smiling speed of light
and how it's all the same story of a small,
hungry umbrella crawling out of a cave,

and even the sky in its violet wealth
does not own a single electron, and yet
there is a balance that maintains
normalcy on a winter Sunday, allowing us
to coagulate here in the holiday

season and laugh at John Gray's
latest scheme while we sway in line
anxiously waiting for something else,
while a tiger in a jungle calls
our name, while the prostitute in silky, red

boredom and the cars plunging through
yellow lights call our name, while the misplaced
magazines and germy doorhandles
call our unspoken name, and a clerk
with a mole on her cheek, and two cups

of coffee anchoring her legs
calls our name, and suddenly
I am next, and step forward alone
into the sunlight of her fluorescent gaze
and relish the strange pollen

of a moment that is mine.

SHIFTING AMBIGUITIES OF SOIL

I.
The relation between respective molds of yogurt and mozzarella,
      having grown within the same refrigerator, only two shelves,
      perhaps five degrees apart.

A hillside near a highway's carving, suddenly flowers with
      determination, the resolve to call your father this year on
      his birthday.

At most hours, the recognition, whenever you leave the supermarket,
      evening sky of pink strata, another enters, mounds of
      cantaloupe, green echoes of bottled wine.

How it lingers, the crescent of light you once let into your room,
      door ajar, and the narrow hallway of temperatures, gaseous
      elements in which life might grow.

Always, at the edges, branches—chattering across synapses,
      interstices of darkness—that seem distant, but grow inside
      the hall, texturing your pillow of stars with bone.

Not the picture, but the scent, the feeling, the negative—of you,
      as soft pine, being braided by large hands, first memories,
      a deck of cards shuffled with moments, with words.

You couldn't comprehend the sadness, the deep sap in their faces,
      hardening. How you redeemed them with almond light,
      pools from wherever you came.

A willow pod, cocoon, seeds you juggled, let fall to earth. Now
      you know what was inside. Cityscapes of desire,
      architectural lust, geometric wheels slicing pink throats of
      birds.

The complexity of earth, how fecundity is more than death. The
massed accumulation of snail feces and paper bills, how
telemarketers might slowly chip away the sky.

Something within life that is not life, that encroaches, expands.
While something you once swore you needed disappears
down the backroads of Kentucky.

Over a bridge, a stream dismantling a dam built by innocence, by
children. Under a moon's repentant stare in which your
father wakes you in the night. With news.

Seventeen caterpillars are dropping from suburban trees in Des
Moines. In each of the houses, each of the rooms, a
different fear has left a light on. And everywhere the smell
of hunger.

Waking, the singular urge to pee and to cover exposure with more
sleep, with earth like a cat's shiftings. Or on the hillside
you suddenly notice flowers, become the sudden flowering.

II.
That the word "sudden" is stitched by our heartbeat. Or flowers.
That we flower faster than flowers. Or think so, but
cannot fathom how quickly a flower's thoughts might flower.

Because, watching rigs rhythmically rape the hillside, the thought of
innocence. Or the innocence of thought. Or the innocent
birds vanishing, braiding the sky with babble, stunning
jewels.

As innocence increases its irrelevance, irrelevance becomes domi-
nant, subsumes the vanishing concepts, the changes in
concepts of change, the conceptual death.

So you walk through the dark and let the leprous textures brush
you, tell you their names. Each day you reach into the icy
spring and insert new eyes.

Slivers of old sight stick to new moons. You finally are taking vows
to floss and call your father on his birthday. It's more than
the surging quiet.

Of moaning that drifted through your room, and out the window,
a space that waited for cardinal, shivering, found some
relief in catching color.

Insistence repeated, a multiplicity of stalks pulsing dirt. The rhyth-
mic elaboration of a hillside, love for what a bare mound
might hide. Therefore, the acrylics.

Of breaking consciousness many times with the importance of
not forgetting. To flower the thought of the day when the
flower must flower, or be noticed flowering.

Because one mold is blue with black edges like a dragonfly's wings,
    the other something of autumn. One breathed first, one
    with more hurry. You grow a grief over the walls between
    them.

The plastic container, the cellophane. Or a grief grows in you,
    spores waiting. You harvest the picture of your father in a
    cold room.

From a cold room? You harvest the acrylics of conscious hymens
    broken many times. You retrieve an extra sweatshirt from
    the car. Drape around his shadow.

Thoughts almost knocking at the door of prayer, you pause *am I
    expected? wanted?* hand frozen, half-raised *maybe she's
    not home,* before turning.

I'll come back keys and coins clearing space before you like a hearse
    later walking away the winding hall, every other door
    wide open.

III.

The texture of the growth is rich as pudenda, and in the rich
   pudenda grows the joy of saying the word pudenda, and
   the joy of mouthing yes.

But also the pleasure of no. In pudenda, the colorings of yogurt
   rich with complaint, the lavender of a savage South
   American bird, feeling her go limp in his arms.

The fertility of effort not to slacken, searching for a glass of
   water in which to cry. And the right chair, a tile with the
   precise gravity of destiny, a merciless pattern.

Israel—to wrestle, because only half the mind hears the vision of
   the pulp inside the birdless branch: that the world's cries
   lubricate the cunt of insatiable beauty.

In pudenda, grows the Israel of pudenda. A single pubic hair as
   both the stroke on which his sister died and the missing
   elevator, the exposed cables of the heart.

Cold stones at the bottom of his eyes. Go ahead: stand in the
   sensual alphabet of times you've stood in streams, roll
   Georgia in your hand like a stone. Plant him there beside
   you.

With words, let the water comb his mind. Reveal the fertility of a
   barren hillside, no one hears the repetition of father's legs
   burning.

The capillaries that flower. Fireworks seen from a hood, in his legs
   the salivating lightning enacting an ordinary and impossible
   revelation. Standing in the uncrippled sound of water.

Looking down, he could feel the sunlight dripping down the backs
    of tulip buds, as you rearranged the rocks below. Sculpting
    the river with your hands of blue wind.

The mountains, looking down, as through glass. You untouched
    touching, the ultimatum of a hawk's figure. Now
    thoughts collide with phone and flower.

Because you've felt the scrape of mountains, not particular, but
    aggregate. You know a text that wants to dissolve, to
    dissolve singing, or to sing dissolution.

That the texture of mountains might also be the scrape on your
    chest. That the mountains are xeroxed in you, but with
    depth, relief. And your text wants to dissolve.

Letters that do not want to flower. Or want to flower in repetition, a
    broad continuity of hillside. Order loosely scattered seeds.
    Wind-borne. Supple to other orders, soil, rains.

You want to call your father with a voice that claims no
    understanding. To insist only on texture. Because you
    know time, you know time, you know time, and how it
    breaks.

IV.

Shortly after cereal. And the lawnmen barbering green. Not to
    transcend, not to compare, nor to desire, and not to reach.
    Not even to move, but to insist.

On love, to live in the texture of. The grain of wood is stream, is
    ocean. But corks your head most uniquely violet. And the
    smell of wet pine helixes memory.

Because he. Or because you. And walls that separate seas cannot.
    Because many thoughts get lost and. Die before. The light.
    Like sperm.

Thoughts that lead the way for others. That die dissolving ovum
    walls, no less cathedral. Minnows threading darkness.
    Swordfish, thoughts that drink the light, they too find
    death.

Something time teaches: to insist. Only on love, in the alchemy
    of substance. Hands touching nothing, intoxicated caresses.
    Barnacles and the thorax of mango-eating insects.

When where is nowhere but blue flowers. Beside red berries
    sculpting the ordinary sun, the afternoon in towers. That
    time teaches all things. Suddenly and slow.

The realization in a field of dust, sunlit, that you have already
    called your father on his birthday, that the flowers flowered,
    almost unnoticed. The rains arriving at their given hours.

And time still blooms in your dresser, your toilet. The molds in
    landfills, still rising. The gulls dissecting the blue and the
    orange. The sun is a ball of squeal.

Toward new murals of insistence, the acrylics crawl. Eyes without
sentences. Hands without syntax, to touch knowingly the
unknown world, a storm in which the butterfly drowns.

But on some measure of love, to insist. To stand in the kitchen,
harvesting winter gourds from cranial peat. To feed flowers
through the phone and cook the onions.

To yes and yes to push ahead of you, coherent shape like an ant, a
spherical estimate, to offer shapes of regard, configured
crumbs of light.

When crossing paths with mirrors, to stop and dance to the nearest
traffic signal. To believe in the dissolving journey of the
sperm, the fluorescent bulbs, the sky asleep within each leaf.

Perpetuate the promise of your son calling you on your birthday.
Long after your repentant moon has hovered over, rippled
his night. With news.

Either we are wrong, or the world. Or the divide is right. Emerging
from the market, to look up and see behind the sun, pain
the only compass, flowering in its silo of bone.

RAIN

I woke up dreaming
of a stranger's empty hands

a desert and a lake, everything
equally rippled by wanting.

I knew I had said too much.

Before you were ever you,
I was you.
           Will that change

the way you touch the yellow peppers
in the supermarket
                    or the currency

you hand over to the face
before you exit.

WALKING

Perhaps because I ordered the vegetarian meal, or because I didn't
bring my seat all the way to the upright position,

the plane drops me off on a landscape of clouds, white kneaded
mountains full of yeast and sunlight

and leaves without allowing me to claim my baggage. Or say
goodbye to the woman I met in line for the bathroom. I am
neither relieved nor disappointed

to find I can walk on the clouds: I am past all that. I am walking.
My steps sink into the liquid marble like white mud, and the sun
installs giant bay windows

on all sides so that it has something to pass through. My eyes feel
unusually welcome, but this is of no concern. I am walking

and the sun is either rising or setting—I don't care which; I am
past all that—the sun is either rising or setting

behind an enormous cloud in the distance, a white mountain that
I do not name though the familiar litany circles like a swarm of
gnats—

Vesuvius, Fuji, Everest, Olympus—and its shape begs to be called
Wolf Howling Mountain, its immensity and color Mountain of
the Winter Goddess.

I am walking and unconcerned. The sun is either rising or setting
behind the mountain, and already the mountain is changing. No
longer a wolf,

now a slight resemblance to a horse leaping from a cliff, its color begins to billow pink rose petals. The mountain is a mystery,

perhaps it holds a chorus of frying pans, perhaps the world's first drop of dew. Either way, my walking does not change. I am past all that.

I am walking, but it is not the walking. Neither the walking nor the changing, nor were I to sit would it be the sitting. Not the shadows

that I am coming toward. And the thin graceful stems of mushrooms that grow in the shadows, not them. Not the pink gasm of light crawling over me

asking me not to leave. Not the tea, set out in my head, steaming, or the table where someone waits. Not the words that funnel space into one point.

I am past all that, I am walking. My feet are tired, but I am unconcerned. Tiny wisps of clouds are beginning to sing, and I am realizing that the sun is rising.

A new day in the white mountains. And I am walking into the sunrise, but it is not the light I am coming toward

or the clouds of cactus that will soon bloom. As it would not have been the dark if the sun had set. As it would not have been the warm night owl of snow.

CODA: FOR WHOM THE BELL TOLLS

Where is the doorway into this impure world?
We are currently experiencing a high volume of calls.
When he turns the faucet on, her blood begins to flow,
the man who lives below them starts to sing.

All morning, the mourning dove. All mourning, the morning.
Your call will be answered in the order it was received.
The bureau of your chest filled with last year's papers;
there are words from here to the end of the world.

So reach out a lace of poplar across a dark continent.
When she turns the wipers on, the sky begins to fall.
Look out the window at one version of mystery.
Who then has lived up to the dignity of a hand?

If you see a woman climbing stairs forever, ignore her.
A wooden laundry basket overflowing with primary hues.
If the stairs are made of metal, if you see her pause
and glance at you, unsung arias condensed to stone, pass on.

Do not worry. The woman changes. She is renewed.
And ask not for what reason she looks at you.
This message will now be repeated twice.
You may exit at any time by pressing zero.

SOURCE

In the bed, a woman dreams.
And through a window, light pours
across her syncopated limbs, strokes
her cheeks that flush and ebb,

except the light is made of hands,
and the hands are really water,
and the water is not water
but what's left after tears

are subtracted from white seeds,
semen, squash wombs, mango,
laughter by the sea, child's toes,
the eyes of crabs, finding one's

body, even briefly,
in the rise of dunes, the ridges
of a shell. The light soothes her
sweat that pools beneath the silk

sheets, furrowed, rippled, writhing;
the hand slows her clock upon
the night stand, and the water
on her forehead writes everything

is well, sculpts the stones she dreams,
sometimes tries to help her wake.
Except there is no night stand,
no earrings, no cup, no clock.

And the walls are made of night,
pure night, starless, and there is
no window through which nothing
pours, no bed, no silk.

There is no starless night
and never has been. Only
a woman turning forever
from side to side, craning her neck,

flailing an arm behind her,
crying, smiling, making fists.
Though, of course, there is no neck
arched through empty space, no rippling,

no woman. But there is the dream.

NOTES TO ORGANIC KNOWING

Ash. Perfection. The stomach growls.
Ebbs, flows. After the birth and death
of every notion. Roses, flowers, cells.
Conversations beside certain trees in which
grew certain desires. Nameless. The name.
The face in the train window of the backward slipping world.
Cupped hands, white sink, or the washing
of the vulva. Wood shavings beneath his work bench.
Crumbs of the unspoken. Everything that was not
love was imagined. And here again, their back
to the camera, two strangers, walking arm in arm,
beneath an umbrella, through Tiannamen Square.

☼

ACKNOWLEDGMENTS

The author wishes to thank the editors of the following publications, in which many of these poems previously appeared:

AGNI: "Coda: For Whom the Bell Tolls"
Bat City Review: "Next,""Background," "Realism: A Landscape of the Body at any Longitude"
The Bitter Oleander: "The Shore," "Source"
Borderlands: Texas Poetry Review: "The Gospel of J," "Sonnet in A Minor," "Notes to Organic Knowing"
The Florida Review: "Anonymous," "John 3:16," "Hologram," "Wedding Song"
Grain: "After Charon: A Late Aubade"
Many Mountains Moving: "Arc"
Mid-American Review: "Accident"
The Midwest Quarterly: "Here in the Mountains"
New Orleans Review: "The Lost World"
Parting Gifts: "Surfacing"
Phoebe: "Postscript"
Poetry International: "The Undressing Room," "Sunday Morning," "Original Sin"
Reactions (UK): "Arc," "The Gospel of J," "After Charon," "Matinée," "Realism: A Landscape of the Body at any Longitude," "Wedding Song," "The Lost World," "John 3:16"
Spoon River Poetry Review: "Waking with Chloe"
Wild Heart Journal: "John 3:16" (reprint)